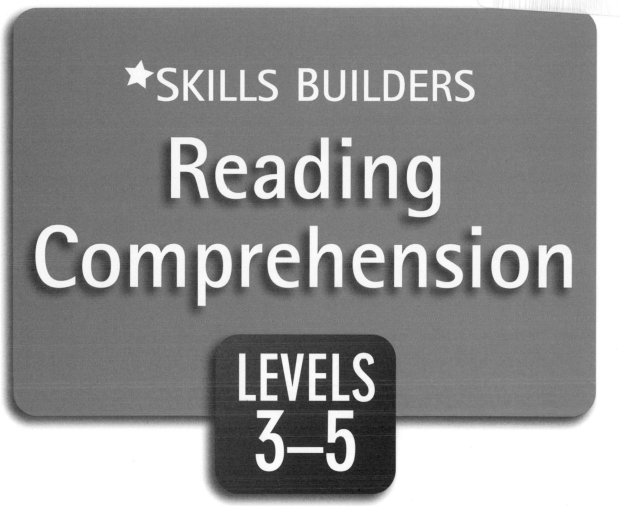

★SKILLS BUILDERS

Reading Comprehension

LEVELS 3–5

Marie Lallaway, Tom Johns and Mig Bennett

RISING★STARS

Rising Stars UK Ltd, 7 Hatchers Mews, Bermondsey Street, London SE1 3GS

www.risingstars-uk.com

Published 2010
Reprinted 2010, 2011

Text, design and layout © 2008 Rising Stars UK Ltd.

Editorial: Marieke O'Connor
Illustrations: Phill Burrows
Design: Branford Graphics and Clive Sutherland
Cover design: Burville-Riley Partnership

Text acknowledgements
pp7 Extract from *Desert Food Chains* by Richard and Louise Spilsbury (top), Extract from *Little Foxes* by Michael Morpurgo, Egmont (bottom); p16 Extract from *The Breadwinner* by Leslie Halward; p17 Extract from *Ramona and Her Mother* by Beverly Cleary (OUP, 2006), copyright © Beverly Cleary 1979, reprinted by permission of Oxford University Press.; p18 HarperCollins Publishers Ltd 2004, Nigel Slater; p20 from *The Lottie Project* by Jacqueline Wilson, published by Doubleday. Reprinted by permission of The Random House Group Ltd.; p21 Extract from *The Truth About Possums* by James Moloney; pp25 HarperCollins Publishers Ltd 2004, Nigel Slater (top), *When Hitler Stole Pink Rabbit* by Judith Kerr (bottom); p27 Extract from *Spilled Water* by Sally Grindley, Bloomsbury; p28 'RSPCA says pets are falling prey to a throwaway society' The Times; p31 Extract from Kiss Kiss "The Landlady" by Roald Dahl. Reproduced by permission of Penguin; p32 Extract from *Wolf* by Gillian Cross (OUP, 2008), copyright © Gillian Cross 1990, reprinted bt permission of Oxford University Press.; p35 *Incendiary* by Vernon Scannell; p36 Text © 1999 Vivian French. Extract from THE BOY WHO WALKED ON WATER AND OTHER STORIES by Vivian French. Reproduced by permission of Walker Books Ltd, London SE11 5MJ; p37 Extract from *Spilled Water* by Sally Grindley, Bloomsbury; pp39 Extract from *Thursday's Child* by Sonya Hartnett (top), Extract from *Neither Here Nor There* by Bill Bryson; p41 *Boy* by Roald Dahl. Reproduced by permission of Jonathon Cape Ltd & Penguin Books Ltd.; p44 Extract from *The Incredible Journey* by Sheila Burnford; p45 Extract from *The Adventures of Tom Sawyer* by Mark Twain.

Picture acknowledgements
p6 Chris Fourie/Dreamstime.com (left), Gjs/Dreamstime.com (right); p7 Photomyeye/Dreamstime.com (left), Olivier Asselin/Alamy (left top centre), Chode/Dreamstime.com (left middle centre) Mel Gama/Dreamstime.com (right top centre), Marek Kosmal/Dreamstime.com (right middle centre), Andreea Ardelean/Dreamstime.com (bottom middle), Tzooka/Dreamstime.com (right); p8 iStockphoto; p11 Frantzesco Kangaris/epa/Corbis; p13 Inspi8ation/Dreamstime.com; p15 Julian Finney/Getty Images; p23 Simon Grosset/Alamy; p28 Andrew Forsyth/RSPCA; p30 Burstein Collection/Corbis.

British Library Cataloguing in Publication Data.
A CIP record for this book is available from the British Library.

ISBN: 978 1 84680 682 7

Printed by Craft Print International Ltd, Singapore

Contents

What are reading skills?

At your age and level, reading is not just about being able to say and understand the words you see. Reading skills include the different ways that you are expected to respond to a text.

These skills are called 'assessment focuses' (AFs) and your teacher considers how well you can perform them when assessing your National Curriculum level for reading.

AF	Teacher speak	This means that you need to:	
2	Understand, describe, select or retrieve information, events or ideas from texts and use quotation and reference to text.	Find and use details of information.	
3	Deduce, infer or interpret information, events or ideas from texts.	Understand what the text 'suggests' but does not directly say.	
4	Identify and comment on the structure and organisation of text, including grammatical and presentational features at text level.	Understand why a text is organised in a particular way.	
5	Explain and comment on writers' use of language, including grammatical and literary features at word and sentence level.	Explain why a writer chooses particular words to create an effect on you, the reader.	
6	Identify and comment on writers' purposes and viewpoints and the overall effect of the text on the reader.	Explain what effect the writer has achieved with the text.	
7	Relate texts to their social, historical and cultural traditions.	Understand what texts show about when and where they were written.	

Why use this book?

This book will help you to move your reading skills up from one National Curriculum level to another. For example, if you are currently working at level 3, advice and exercises will help you to progress to level 4, or 5.

- **Knowing what you need to do** to achieve your target level is also essential so we explain and give examples of what you need to be able to do.
- We know that students **learn by doing** so practice is an important part of the book.

The book includes the following features to make it easy to use and to highlight what you really need to be able to do.

Target level statement – this tells you what you need to do to achieve the next level in your reading skill.

Assessment focus – this identifies the main reading skill that is being practised. See page 5 for more information.

Tips – these give you helpful hints, similar to how your teacher does in class.

Practice questions – lots of short fiction and non-fiction texts with guided questions for you to practise with and build your skills and confidence in reading.

How to use this book

- You can use the sections in this book to work on the reading skills you need to practise. Or, work through the whole book for overall improvement.

★ Ask your teacher for advice on which reading skills to practise first.
Your teacher will be pleased you are making a special effort to improve!

- Each section targets a different reading skill and allows you to practise the skill in a variety of ways across levels 3, 4 and 5 so that you can learn the 'extra' things you need to understand and do for each level.

- Practise in short bursts of activity and **do** read the advice first so that you focus on the reading skill, not just answering the questions.

★ 'Warm up' by doing an exercise at your current reading level before trying the exercises to move you up to the next level.

- Continue your practice by thinking of your own questions about the things you read outside of this book. For example, when reading a news article, think about what you could ask someone else about it.

Use this table to identify what you want to do first.

Reading skills	Find and use details of information	Understand what the text 'suggests' but does not directly say	Understand why a text is organised in a particular way	Explain why a writer chooses particular words to create an effect on you, the reader	Explain what effect the writer has achieved with the text
Level 3	from short sections of text	understand some of the writer's 'simple' meanings	identify simple features of text organisation	identify simple language features	identify the main purpose of a text
Level 4	in selected areas of longer texts	understand the writer's meanings and explain them simply	identify the basic overall organisation of a text	identify and make simple comments about interesting language	identify and make simple comments about the purpose of a text
Level 5	from larger amounts of text and use details as evidence to support opinions	explain the writer's meanings in your own words	identify the pattern of ideas in a text and make comments about it	identify and comment on the effects of interesting language	identify the purpose of a text and begin to explain its effect on the reader

★ Shade each box when you have done the exercises correctly to record your progress.

Finding information in a text

> Level 3 readers can find information from short sections of text.
> **Level 4 readers can find information in short texts, or selected areas of longer texts.**

TIP   ★   When looking for information, read the text first, then read the question, then read the text again to look for the answer (even if you think you know it!).

1 Read this text and highlight at least three things an elephant uses its trunk to do.

> The most distinctive feature of an elephant is its trunk. The elephant uses it to breathe and smell, as well as to pick up food and water.
>
> An elephant can suck up 55 litres of water at a time through its trunk.

2 Check the information in this text and draw lines to link the information in the boxes below to the correct elephant.

> African and Asian elephants are not quite the same. African elephants are larger than Asian elephants and they have bigger ears. African elephants' ears are fan-shaped and can be as big as 1.5 metres.
>
> Asian elephants have smaller ears, triangular in shape. Their trunks are different, too. The Asian elephant has just one lip at the end of its trunk. The African elephant has two.

fan-shaped ears   one lip on trunk

African elephant   triangular ears   two lips on trunk   **Asian elephant**

ears up to 1.5 m wide   smaller type of elephant

TIP

★ Remember: TEXT ➡ QUESTION ➡ TEXT
Don't miss out any stage!

3 Read this text and draw lines from the animals to the food they eat.

Desert Dogs

Several kinds of wild dogs live in deserts. The fennec fox has large ears that help it hear prey animals such as insects and lizards in the dark. Jackals, such as the black-backed jackal, are omnivores. They eat grasses and fruits, and also scavenge chunks of flesh from dead animals.

Desert Food Chains by Richard and Louise Spilsbury

Jackal

Fennec fox

4 Read this text and answer the questions below. In this story, a young boy brings a new pet back to the house he lives in with his aunt.

'What's that you're hiding there, Billy? Show me, show me at once.' And she took Billy by the shoulder and swung him round to face her. Billy expected her to scream but she did not. Her mouth gaped in horror as she backed away from him, knocking over the kitchen stool behind her. 'Get that thing out of here,' she whispered. 'Get it out. Billy, either you put that thing out of that door this minute or … or … Billy, either it goes at once, or you both go. Do you understand me, Billy? Do you understand what I'm saying?'

'Yes, Aunty May,' said Billy. And with the fox cradled against him he walked to the front door and opened it. 'Goodbye,' he said, and he was gone before she could collect herself.

Little Foxes by Michael Morpurgo

a) Did Aunty May scream? _____

b) What did she knock over? _____

c) What was Billy hiding? _____

d) What did he do at the end of the story? _____

Level 3 readers can find information from short sections of text.
Level 4 readers can find information in short texts, or selected areas of longer texts.

5 Read this text about pasta and fill in the gaps in the task that follows.

If you are new to cooking, pasta will probably be one of the first things you learn to cook. University students say it is their perfect food – quick to cook and cheap to buy. It is made from just flour, water and salt but some types also contain eggs. Though it is easy to cook you have to get the timing right. Overcooked pasta leads to an unpleasant glue-like meal.

a) _____ students eat a lot of pasta because it is b) _____ and

c) _____ . Pasta sometimes contains eggs but usually it is just water,

d) _____ and e) _____ .

6 Read this menu and answer the questions that follow.

Today's specials

Chargrilled peppers and baked onions in a tomato pasta
or Kashmir turkey curry with wild rice and an onion relish

Vegetables

Baby new carrots with parsley
Steamed broccoli
Green beans cooked with walnuts

Dessert

Apple pie and thick brandy-flavoured cream
New York cheesecake
Banana ice cream with chocolate sauce

a) Circle these answers on the menu.

   i) What is served with wild rice?

   ii) Which vegetable is steamed?

   iii) What flavour is the pie?

b) Tick the food on the menu that you want to order.

   i) You had curry yesterday and you want a change.

   ii) You don't want broccoli or beans.

   iii) You love chocolate.

TIP ★ Identify and highlight key words while you read.

7 Read the script below. Draw lines to match each boy with the type of pizza he ate.

> **Nick:** I went to the pizza place on Sunday with Abdul and Charlie. It was great. Have you been, Tom?
>
> **Tom:** Yes, I've been there. I had the Three Cheese Pizza.
>
> **Nick:** I had the Hot and Spicy one. My mate Charlie had it too. You should try it.
>
> **Tom:** What, me? No, I don't do hot and spicy stuff. I'd rather eat nothing!
>
> **Nick:** Abdul wouldn't eat it either. He just had plain Cheese and Tomato.

Charlie   **Abdul**   **Tom**   **Nick**

8 Read the news report to find the information. Then fill in the gaps below.

> **Adverts for foods high in fat, salt and sugar have been banned during television programmes aimed at children under 16, in an effort to tackle obesity levels in children.**
>
>
>
> But programme makers say the quality of children's programmes will suffer because they will lose an estimated £39 million in advertising income.
>
> Health campaigners had called for a complete ban before the 9 p.m. watershed.
>
> The move is the latest stage in a crackdown on junk food advertising during programmes aimed at, or appealing to, children.

a) The ban is aimed at children aged _____ .

b) The ban is on foods containing a lot of _____ , _____ and

_____ .

c) Programme makers may lose about £_____ .

d) Campaigners want to stop the advertising of _____ before _____ p.m. at night.

Level 4 readers can find information in short texts, or selected areas of longer texts.

Level 5 readers can find information from larger amounts of text, and find evidence to support opinions.

Always read a text once to get a general idea. Then read it again, focusing on finding out what you need to know.

TIP ★ Use a highlighter pen to target points in the text that will help you with the answers.

9 This advert for a DVD rental company has a lot of information to persuade people to use their service.

> # FILMS FOR FREE
> ## FREE TRIAL AND CINEMA TICKETS
>
> LOVEFiLM is the UK's biggest and best online DVD rental service, delivering DVDs to your door. The site carries 65,000-plus titles, including games and a downloads service. Try the service for free and then become a full member by choosing one of our rental packages. Prices start from £3.99 a month for a 'capped' package and £9.99 a month for an 'unlimited' package. LOVEFiLM's unlimited packages allow you to watch as many DVDs as you like, with free postage both ways and no late fees.
>
> To redeem this offer, visit lovefilm.com and enter the code NW3CN2.
>
> Expires 27 June.

lots to choose from

a) Highlight **five** good things mentioned in this advert to attract customers.

b) Add labels and write what you think is good about them. An example has been done for you.

10 Read this short magazine article about Daniel Craig.

Daniel Craig, the new James Bond, told his personal trainer that he had to 'look like I could kill someone when I take my shirt off' when he started to prepare for his new role as 007 James Bond.

He gave up smoking, exercised five times a week and stopped drinking beer every day. His workouts lasted about 45 minutes but they were hard. His trainer was an ex-Royal Marine soldier who really put him through his paces. He hadn't done much gym work before. He needed to be fit, not so much because he needed to look good, but because he had to be able to do the stunts and the very many complicated fight sequences. This wasn't his normal work. And as for looking good – he achieved that too!

a) Find four changes Daniel Craig made to his life while preparing for his role as James Bond. Quote from the text to give the evidence for your answer. An example has been done for you.

Change	Evidence
stopped smoking	gave up smoking

b) Give two reasons why Daniel Craig did this training.

TIP   ★ Don't forget the highlighter!

TIP ★ Read a text right through once to get a general idea. Then read the question and find the answers. DON'T try to just remember them.

11 In this story, two teenagers meet in the park.

Tina is pushing her small cousin on the swing in the park.

A boy appears and wanders towards the roundabout, sits on it and takes out a phone. She hears him talking to someone.

He jumps off the roundabout, leaps over the end of the slide and comes to swing casually on a tyre hanging nearby.

'I know you, don't I?' she says.

The boy blushes. 'You're in my science class.' 'Yeah, I remember. It was you who nearly blew the place up, wasn't it? On Friday?'

The boy twists the tyre round and lets it go. 'Sort of. But it was an accident.' He jumps off the tyre. 'Got a trip to the Head's office for that one.'

'Do accidents follow you around then?' asks Tina. 'You were the one who dropped a tray of food in the canteen, last week.'

The boy goes red. 'Yep, you weren't the only one who enjoyed that show. I slipped on the beans too – Head suggested I apply to be a circus clown.'

Tina laughs. 'You're all right, really, aren't you! Gavin Tubb, isn't it?' The boy looks pleased. 'Yeah. I'll walk back with you if you like.'

a) Find two places Tina has seen Gavin before.

b) Find three accidents Gavin has had.

c) Find four pieces of play equipment.

12 This news report is about a music tour by a singer called Jacinta.

Jacinta's tour to start off in UK

Jacinta will perform in a number of major cities.

Pop superstar Jacinta has announced that she will launch her 20-date world tour in Sheffield on 24 August.

The 'Sun and Sand' tour will start at the Hallam Arena, winding up in Chicago on 29 November.

Tickets go on sale from 10.00 a.m. on 15 May with prices for the Sheffield show starting at £35.

The tour will cover many cities across Europe, including Paris, Rome and Berlin, as well as cities in America.

Her last tour was in 2005. More than 1.1 million people went to her shows at venues across the world which makes it the highest-earning concert tour by a female singer at the time.

Her recent album, 'Emotional Avenue', has charted at number one in 12 countries so far, including the UK, France, Germany, Japan and Australia, according to her record company.

a) Fill in the details.

i)	Tour name	
ii)	Tour starts – when/where	
iii)	Tour ends – when/where	
iv)	Cheapest ticket price	
v)	How many people saw last tour	
vi)	Name of album	

b) Double check your answers by highlighting the evidence in the article.

c) Write a paragraph explaining how you can tell that Jacinta is really successful. Use at least five pieces of evidence from the article to support your answer.

> **TIP**
> ★ Decide which evidence you will use **before** you start writing.

Understanding what the writer 'suggests'

Level 3 readers can understand some of the writer's simple meanings.
Level 4 readers can understand the writer's meanings, and explain them simply.

★ In questions, the word 'suggest' means you have to understand what the writer is telling you without actually saying it.

1 In these sentences the writer uses words to *suggest* something about the people in the text. What does the bold phrase suggest? Circle two possible answers for each.

a) Lori gave Josh a **weak smile** and then turned away.

Lori is **happy   sad   angry   disappointed**.

b) It was hard work walking in that heat with Marco **leaning on her arm** all the time.

Marco is **old   injured   glad   unkind**.

c) My brother Simon **did a disappearing act** when there were jobs to be done.

Simon is **lazy   a magician   crafty   hard-working**.

★ Sometimes you have to look at more than one clue for the right answer.

2 Which answer do *all* the bold clues suggest to you? Circle one answer.

a) Mum **banged the plates down** on the table, her **lips tight**, her eyes **narrowed** and her **movements brisk**.

Mum is **busy   worried   angry**.

b) Harry's **steps felt light** as he left Marnie at the bus stop. She'd said 'Yes'. She was coming with him to his match tomorrow. He **grinned broadly** and **laughed**.

Harry is **pleased about something   thinks something is funny   is being spiteful**.

c) The tiger **swished its tail** back and forth as it **crouched down** before him. Its **lips curled** back slightly from its teeth and its **eyes held a steady stare**.

The tiger is **playful   about to attack   in pain**.

★ Do not just repeat the words the writer has used. Look for what they *suggest*.

14

TIP

★ Always make sure you have some 'evidence' for your answers.

3 Read this extract from a teenager's diary. Look for clues to help you do the task below.

> **Luke's diary**
>
> Bad weather so I expected football coaching to be off. But, luckily, it wasn't. Danny was on top form. I'm sure he can't remember all our names because he calls everyone 'dude'. I asked him about it once and he agreed that I was right – but it's funny because he can always remember which football teams we support. Although he is a bit of a nutcase, he is an excellent coach. My game has really improved. But his jokes – they are seriously no good.

Tick whether these are True or False and then highlight the phrases above that helped you to find the True answers. This text *suggests* that …

a) Luke is pleased to be going to football.   **True** ☐   **False** ☐

b) Luke enjoys Danny's jokes.   **True** ☐   **False** ☐

c) Danny forgets everyone's names.   **True** ☐   **False** ☐

d) Danny is very good at his job.   **True** ☐   **False** ☐

TIP

★ A **phrase** is more than one word.

4 Read this text about a tennis player and answer the questions below.

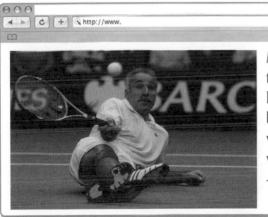

Mansour Bahrami is the most entertaining tennis player of all time – the joker of the tennis world. His skilful trick shots have the crowd applauding and cheering. Serving with six balls in his hand, playing whilst sitting in a chair, play-acting with his doubles partner and pretending to have arguments with his opponents are only a few of his antics …

Tennis is never dull when the clown prince takes to the court.

a) Find three **words** that *suggest* people like to watch Bahrami play tennis.

_____   _____   _____

b) Find two **phrases** used to describe Bahrami that *suggest* he is funny.

_____

_____

Level 3 readers can understand some of the writer's simple meanings.

Level 4 readers can understand the writer's meanings, and explain them simply.

5 Read this short text. The writer of this piece gives an impression, rather than saying something directly. Find the correct words or phrases and write them in the table.

> We piled out of the bus, charged up the steps and beamed at Mum as she opened the door. The holiday was over at last.

The writer wants you to know that ...	Which word or phrase suggests this?
a) the children were hurrying	
b) the children were pleased	
c) the holiday had not been good	

TIP

★ Do not just repeat the words the writer has used. Look for what they *suggest*.

6 Read this text from a leaflet about a theme park. What is the writer suggesting? Tick the correct answer.

> First things first, remember it's a whole day! Not a couple of hours or a few minutes. You have an entire day to enjoy the mass of magical entertainment ahead of you.

☐ A day is not enough time to do everything.

☐ Don't rush because you have plenty of time in a day's visit.

☐ It only takes a few minutes to do each thing.

☐ It is the best day you will ever have.

7 Read this extract from a story about a boy in trouble with his father. Highlight the **phrase** which *suggests* that the father is behaving like a fierce animal.

> The father advanced on the boy, his teeth showing in a snarl under his big moustache.
> 'Where's the money?' he almost whispered.
> 'I lost it,' he said.
> 'You – what?' cried the father.
> 'I lost it,' the boy repeated.
> The man began to shout and wave his hands about.
> 'Lost it! Lost it! What are you talking about? How could you lose it?'
>
> *The Breadwinner* by Leslie Halward

TIP ★ A **phrase** is more than one word and less than a full sentence, e.g. *The man began to shout and wave his hands about.*

8 Read this story and answer the questions below. A young girl called Ramona tells her parents and brother she is going to run away.

> Ramona made up her mind to shock her parents, really shock them.
>
> 'I am going to run away,' she announced.
>
> 'I'm sorry to hear that,' said Mr Quimby.
>
> 'When are you leaving?' enquired Ramona's mother politely.
>
> The question was almost more than Ramona could bear. Her mother was supposed to say, Oh Ramona, please, please don't leave me!
>
> 'Today,' Ramona managed to say with quivering lips. 'This morning.'
>
> 'She just wants you to feel sorry for her,' said heartless Beezus. 'She wants you to stop her.'
>
> Ramona waited for her mother or father to say something, but neither spoke. Finally there was nothing for Ramona to do but get up from the couch. 'I guess I'll go pack,' she said, and started towards her room.
>
> *Ramona and Her Mother* by Beverly Cleary

a) Circle the correct phrase to fill the gap.

The writer suggests that Ramona _____ to run away.

is determined   is happy   doesn't really want   is desperate

b) Highlight clues in the text that explain *why* you think this.

c) The writer suggests that Ramona's parents are _____ .

cruel to her   shocked by her   used to her   worried about her

d) Highlight clues in the text that explain *why* you think this.

e) Highlight two **phrases** in the text that suggest that Ramona is very upset.

f) The word _____ suggests Beezus doesn't care about Ramona's feelings.

TIP ★ Use your own words to explain what the text suggests to you.

9 Write an instruction to tell your friend how to find out what the writer is suggesting in a text, e.g. Look for … and … that give you … .

_____

_____

_____

Level 4 readers can understand some of the writer's meanings, but often explain them using the writer's words.

Level 5 readers can understand the writer's meanings and explain them in their own words.

10 In this autobiography, the writer remembers a moment from his childhood.

> My mother is scraping a piece of burned toast out of the kitchen window, a crease of annoyance across her forehead. This is not an occasional occurrence, a once-in-a-while hiccup in a busy mother's day. My mother burns the toast as surely as the sun rises each morning. In fact, I doubt if she has ever made a round of toast in her life that failed to fill the kitchen with plumes of throat-catching smoke. I am nine now and have never seen butter without black bits in it.
>
> It is impossible not to love someone who makes toast for you. As your teeth break through the rough, toasted crust and sink into the doughy cushion of white bread and the warm salty butter has hit your tongue, you are smitten.
>
> *Toast* by Nigel Slater

a) True or False? Tick your answers.

   i)   Mother throws away the toast.   True ☐   False ☐

   ii) The sun is rising.   True ☐   False ☐

   iii) Mother always burns the toast.   True ☐   False ☐

   iv) There are bits of burnt bread in the butter.   True ☐   False ☐

b) Highlight the evidence in the text for any of the statements in part **a)** that you think are true.

c) *It is impossible not to love someone who makes toast for you.*
   What does this quotation suggest about the boy's relationship with his mother?

TIP ★ When you think you understand the writer's meaning, go back and check it makes sense with the whole text.

11 This story is about girls' football. Two boys are watching them play.

Bert and Wayne stood together on the sidelines and watched the girls' teams kick off.

'This is going to be rubbish. I don't want to watch a load of girls,' moaned Wayne, taking out his mobile and checking his messages.

'Well, there you're wrong. Watch Bella, number seven. She's a legend. Scored more goals than you this season, that's a fact,' said Bert, his eyes on the game.

'It'll be about as gripping as a Spanish lesson – you just rate Bella and any excuse to see her. I know you!' laughed Wayne sarcastically, his eyes fixed on his mobile screen.

'Well, who wouldn't?' replied Bert, dreamily, his eyes firmly fixed on number seven.

'I wouldn't, that I can ...,' began Wayne, looking up, only to be interrupted by a shout from his friend.

'Wow! Magic! Straight into the corner.' Bert yelled.

'... Right. Yeah, ... awesome.' Wayne stared at Bella in disbelief and shook his head. 'Not bad for a girl. ... Should have laid it off to the winger really – she was in a better position.'

Bert smiled to himself. It was good to be right, for once.

a) Complete this table to explain what the writer suggests about the characters of Bert and Wayne.

	The writer suggests he ...	Evidence from the text
Bert		
Wayne		

TIP ★ Use your own words to explain your ideas.

b) What do you learn about Bert and Wayne in this text?

Practise writing up your comments in your own words by answering this question in one paragraph.

TIP ★ The word 'suggest' means you have to work out what the writer means but doesn't actually say.

Sue didn't like Jenny. ➤➤ **means that** ➤➤ **Sue didn't like Jenny.**

Sue scowled at Jenny. ➤➤ **could suggest that** ➤➤ **Sue didn't like Jenny.**

12 In this story, a schoolgirl, Charlie, describes the arrival of a new teacher.

Miss Beckworth. She was new so I thought she'd be young. When you get a new teacher they're often ever so strict the first few weeks just to show you who's boss, and then they relax and get all friendly. Then you can muck about and do whatever you want.

I *love* fooling around, doing crazy things and being a bit sassy* and making everyone laugh. Even the teachers. But the moment I set eyes on Miss

Beckworth I knew none of us were going to be laughing. She might be new but she certainly wasn't young ...

There are some teachers – just a few – who have YOU'D BETTER NOT MESS WITH ME! tattooed right across their foreheads. She frowned at me with this incredibly fierce forehead and said, 'Good morning. This isn't a very good start to the new school year.'

sassy – cheeky, rude, disrespectful

The Lottie Project by Jacqueline Wilson

a) True or False? Tick your answer.

   i) Charlie usually knows how to handle new teachers.   **True** ☐   **False** ☐

   ii) Charlie doesn't like most teachers.   **True** ☐   **False** ☐

   iii) Some teachers find Charlie fun.   **True** ☐   **False** ☐

   iv) Miss Beckworth has a tattoo.   **True** ☐   **False** ☐

   v) Miss Beckworth is strict.   **True** ☐   **False** ☐

b) Highlight the evidence in the text for any of the statements above that you think are true.

13 In this story, the writer tells us of a conversation about cats between her father and their neighbour, Mrs Waller.

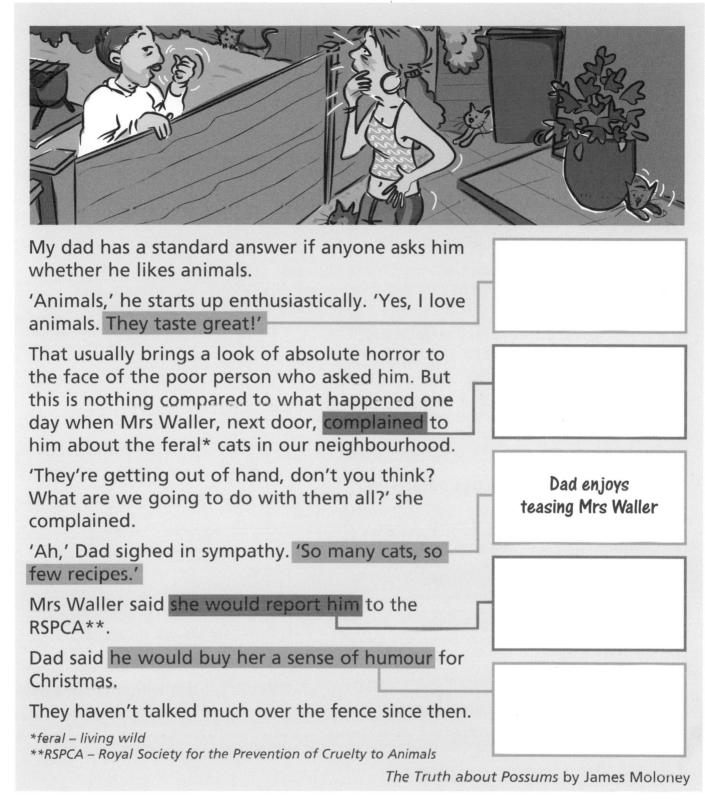

My dad has a standard answer if anyone asks him whether he likes animals.

'Animals,' he starts up enthusiastically. 'Yes, I love animals. They taste great!'

That usually brings a look of absolute horror to the face of the poor person who asked him. But this is nothing compared to what happened one day when Mrs Waller, next door, complained to him about the feral* cats in our neighbourhood.

'They're getting out of hand, don't you think? What are we going to do with them all?' she complained.

'Ah,' Dad sighed in sympathy. 'So many cats, so few recipes.'

Mrs Waller said she would report him to the RSPCA**.

Dad said he would buy her a sense of humour for Christmas.

They haven't talked much over the fence since then.

*feral – living wild
**RSPCA – Royal Society for the Prevention of Cruelty to Animals

Dad enjoys teasing Mrs Waller

The Truth about Possums by James Moloney

a) Write in the boxes what you learn about Dad and Mrs Waller from the highlighted parts of the story. An example has been done for you.

b) Explain, in one paragraph, what you learn about Dad and Mrs Waller. Use quotations as evidence for your comments.

TIP

★ At Level 5, readers can **explain** what the text **suggests** to them.

Commenting on the organisation of texts

Level 3 readers can identify some simple features of text organisation.
Level 4 readers can identify the basic overall organisation of a text.

Writers *choose* the overall pattern of their work to have the best effect on a reader.

1 The writer of this horoscope has used colour to organise the text. Fill in the boxes with these labels:

love life　　title　　action – what to do　　sub-title

Aquarius Jan 20–Feb 18

Life: You are trying too hard – just be yourself and people will love you as you are.

Love: Bored with the usual boys? Try looking in places you never thought to look.

Friends: Plan a girls' night – invite your best friends over for a girlie DVD, then get out the make-up and transform yourselves into the stars.

Capricorn Dec 22–Jan 19

Life: You will have to let others win this month – you can't always have it your own way.

Love: Look out! The guy for you might be someone you already know.

Friends: Do something positive! Raise money for a charity, organise a party – get out there!

a

b

c

d

2 Write the next horoscope for Libra (September 23–October 22) following the same pattern as you have found in the ones above.

3 Read this text. Describe what happens in each section by matching the labels and drawing lines to the right section. One has been done for you.

offers hope

describes suffering

Goodbye, Loyal Little Donkey?

quickly catches reader's attention

Day after day, this little donkey had to march miles along busy, dangerous roads so his owner could feed his family. Carrying a heavy load, it was only a matter of time before he stumbled and fell.

gives a promise

Without our organisation, horses and donkeys around the world would be left to die by the roadside. Now we desperately need your help to pay for the cost of our mobile animal hospitals – bringing urgent help to suffering animals.

£25 COULD PAY FOR EMERGENCY TREATMENTS FOR 50 ANIMALS.

asks for money

Your gift will be spent treating working horses and donkeys, where the need is greatest.

TIP
★ Looking at the 'job' of each section helps you to understand the organisation of a text.

4 Find a leaflet of your own. Identify the 'job' of each section.

Level 3 readers can identify some simple features of text organisation.
Level 4 readers can identify the basic overall organisation of a text.

TIP ★ If the writing focuses on one thing and then moves to another, the writer *chooses* to organise it this way. Look out for any **changes** in the text. Think about why they happen.

5 These two texts describe going to a theme park. Which description do you like the best?

Up, down, round and round. The fun was never-ending. Then I was sick.

Tom

I was sick after going on lots of rides. It was really good fun going up and down, round and round.

Kirsty

6 Show how each description is organised by filling in the gaps.

a) Tom's description:

First of all, he describes _____. Then he tells you

_____.

b) Kirsty's description:

First of all, she describes _____. Then she tells you

_____.

c) I prefer _____'s description because _____.

7 a) Write a three-sentence account of a disastrous event, giving the ending first.

_____

_____

_____

b) Write about the same event but give the ending last.

_____

_____

_____

8 Read this description of a painful event and answer the questions.

> One day my father came home from work, and even before he had taken off his coat he grabbed one of our jam tarts from the wire cooling rack. He couldn't have known they had come from the oven only a minute or two before. His hands flapped, his face turned a deep raspberry red, beads of sweat formed like warts on his brow, he danced a merry dance. As he tried to swallow and his eyes filled with the sort of tears a man can only summon when he has boiling lemon curd stuck to the roof of his mouth, I am sure that I saw the faintest of smiles flicker across my mother's face.
>
> *Toast* by Nigel Slater

a) Who is the writer concentrating on for most of the text?

b) Who is the writer concentrating on at the end?

c) Why has the writer *chosen* to change the person he is concentrating on?

> **TIP**
> ★ In a text about characters, look out for changes in the character that the writer is concentrating on.

9 Read this extract from a story about Mama, Max and Anna. They are trying to escape on a train during the Second World War. The passport inspector comes to their compartment.

> He looked at the passport of the lady with the basket, nodded, stamped it with a little rubber stamp, and gave it back to her.
>
> Then he turned to Mama. Mama handed him the passports and smiled. But the hand with which she was holding her handbag was squeezing it into terrible contortions. The man examined the passports. Then he looked at Mama to see if it was the same face as on the passport photograph, then at Max and then at Anna. Then he got out his rubber stamp. Then he remembered something and looked at the passports again. Then at last he stamped them and gave them back to Mama.
>
> 'Pleasant journey,' he said as he opened the door of the compartment.
>
> *When Hitler Stole Pink Rabbit* by Judith Kerr

a) Most of this text focuses on the passport inspector but some of it focuses on Mama. Highlight the sentences which focus on Mama.

b) Read the text without the sentences focusing on Mama. Now, explain why the writer chose to put those sentences in the middle of this section.

> **TIP**
> ★ The person the writer concentrates on is the **focus** of attention, like a camera lens **focuses** on a particular object.

Level 4 readers can identify the basic organisation of a text.

Level 5 readers can identify the pattern of ideas in a text and make comments about it.

It is useful to look at the opening and the ending of the text to find out what they do.

Writers have a mental map of their work. The reader needs to understand that map.

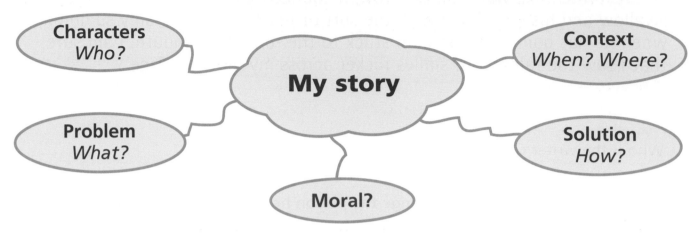

An ending may be a surprise to YOU, but that is because the WRITER has planned it that way!

10 What do openings do? Tick True or False.

    a) Introduce characters   **True** ☐   **False** ☐

    b) Describe locations   **True** ☐   **False** ☐

    c) Give an opinion   **True** ☐   **False** ☐

    d) Make a statement   **True** ☐   **False** ☐

    e) Ask a question   **True** ☐   **False** ☐

Yes, that was a trick question. Openings can do almost anything. Understanding WHY a writer chooses an opening is the challenge!

11 What kinds of endings are these? Label the sentences with these types of endings.

          cliff hanger   **summary**   **request**

    a) All in all, everyone had a wonderful day at the theme park: eating ice cream, enjoying the rides and getting soaked!

    b) Who knows whether the ghost will walk again?

    c) Will you get involved and help us to make a change?

TIP ★ Explain clearly how the ending fits the text. You need to do more than add a label!

12 This story is set in China, long ago. It is about Lu Si-yan, a Chinese girl, whose father has died. She lives with her mother and her Uncle Ba. They are very poor.

Chapter One: To Market

I loved my baby brother, until Uncle took me to market and sold me. He was the bright, shiny pebble in the water, the twinkling star in the sky. Until Uncle took me to market and sold me. Then I hated him.

'Lu Si-yan,' Uncle greeted me early one summer morning, 'today is a big day for you. From today, you must learn to find your own way in the muddy whirlpool of life. Your mother and I have given you a good start. Now it is your turn.'

My mother stood in the shadows of our kitchen, but she didn't look at me and she didn't say a word. Uncle took me tightly by the wrist. As he led me from the house, my mother reached out her hand towards me and clawed the air as though trying to pull me back. Then she picked up my little brother and hid behind the door, but I saw her face wither with pain and, in that moment, fear gripped my heart.

'Where are you taking me, Uncle Ba?' I cried.

'It's for the best,' he replied, his mouth set grimly.

'You're hurting my arm,' I cried.

He pulled me past the scorched patchwork terraces of my family's smallholding, scattering hens and ducks along the way, and out on to the dusty track that led steeply up to the road. There, we walked, Uncle brisk and businesslike, me dragging my feet in protest, until we came to the bus-stop.

'Where are we going, Uncle Ba?' I whimpered this time.

'To market,' he said.

Spilled Water by Sally Grindley, Bloomsbury

a)   What kind of ending is this?

cliff hanger   **summary**   **request**

b)   Explain why you think this.

c)   How does the opening paragraph link to the ending of the chapter?

d)   Most of the chapter is about Lu Si-yan and her uncle. Why does the writer add a paragraph about her mother in the middle of this section?

TIP

★   DO NOT tell the story. Think about how it is organised.

Practise working with a longer text in this task. Read this article.

RSPCA says pets are falling prey to a throwaway society

Valerie Elliott, Countryside Editor

1 The number of pets being abandoned by owners in the UK has grown by almost 25 per cent in a year, raising concern that animals are the latest victims of a 'throwaway society'.

2 Figures from the RSPCA, the country's biggest animal welfare charity, also show that half of the 7,347 animals rescued from the streets last year were cats.

3 The trend is particularly disturbing because cats have traditionally been thought of as relatively easy to care for. They can be let out into a garden without supervision whereas dogs require daily exercise. Nine million people own cats in Britain, compared with 6.5 million who have dogs. The RSPCA is concerned that people are ready to give up their pets for the most bizarre reasons. One owner told an inspector: 'My cat doesn't match my new carpet.' Another said: 'I've just bought a new leather sofa and I don't want the cat to scratch it.'

4 Dogs and rabbits are also being discarded by their owners. Animal officers employed by local authorities have reported that animals are routinely abandoned when owners go on holiday. Pets are turned out on the streets for two weeks and then owners often wish to reclaim them on their return.

5 The RSPCA says the trend shows no sign of diminishing. In the first four months of this year the charity has rescued 2,621 abandoned animals.

6 Two weeks ago, a three-legged cat with no tail was dumped in Portishead, near Bristol. The cat, named Harry, was microchipped so the RSPCA could find out his details. His owners had moved house and inspectors are trying to trace them while the cat is being cared for at a home. Other dumpings last year included a litter of kittens found in a refuse bag in London; a rabbit abandoned in a box in a crushing machine at a recycling centre ... a puppy left in an empty chocolate box ...

7 Tim Wass, chief officer of the RSPCA Inspectorate, said: 'It is an offence to abandon an animal and there is never any excuse for doing so. If people have pets they cannot care for, for any reason, then help and advice is always available from the RSPCA.'

13 Look at how the ideas change from paragraph to paragraph.

Complete this table to show what kind of information each paragraph contains.

Paragraph number	Statistical evidence	Real-life examples	Other
1	✓		
2			
3			
4		✓	
5			
6			
7			

14 How does the opening of the article prepare the reader for what it is about?

15 Why has the writer broken up the statistical evidence with real-life examples?

16 How does the ending link to the opening of the article?

17 Why has the writer used some shorter paragraphs and some longer paragraphs?

TIP

★ Always check how the ending links back to the opening, or how it contrasts with it.

Commenting on how a writer uses language for effect

Level 3 readers can identify simple language features.

Level 4 readers can identify interesting language and make simple comments about it.

1 Choose some words to help you to describe this picture.

painful

2 Read this short paragraph about a man on a train. Put the red words and phrases into three groups in the table below to show how they help to build up an impression of the man.

> The man in the seat opposite to me had a **button nose** and **small, piggy eyes**. He was **well-dressed** in a **smart pin-stripe suit** but his tie was **frayed** and **stained**. The newspaper he had opened at the start of the journey was **still unread**, as he kept looking around him **anxiously**, as if expecting someone else to arrive.

Positive impression	Negative impression	Neutral impression

TIP

★ *Similar ... but different ...*
Words can be quite similar, but their effect is different. You need to begin to recognise differences between words.

3 Explain the difference between the following pairs of words.
   a) BULLYING and BOSSY
   b) HOUSE and HOME

★ Writers *choose* each word they use. They *choose* the word so that it has a particular *effect* on the reader. The word will suggest ideas to the reader.

Think about what the word *suggests* to you as well as what it **means**.

4 What creature, person and natural power do you associate with the words in the table below? Fill in the table following the examples given.

Word	Animal	Person	Natural power
roar	lion	army sergeant shouting at troops	waves crashing into a cave on the seashore
thunder			
bark			
whine			

5 This is the beginning of a Roald Dahl story, *The Landlady*. A young man arrives in a new town. Read the extract and answer the questions.

Billy Weaver had travelled down from London on the slow afternoon train with a change at Swindon on the way, and by the time he got to Bath it was about 9 o'clock in the evening and the moon was coming up out of a clear starry sky over the houses opposite the station entrance. But the air was deadly cold and the wind was like a flat blade of ice on his cheeks.

a) The writer could have used 'very cold' instead of 'deadly cold'. 'Deadly' is a better choice

because it suggests _____.

b) The writer could have used 'the wind was like ice'. 'Like a flat blade of ice' is better

because it suggests _____.

Level 3 readers can identify simple language features.
Level 4 readers can identify interesting language and make simple comments about it.

Writers make lots of choices. The length of a sentence can have an effect on the reader, so writers sometimes choose to use short sentences. Short sentences never appear by accident. They always have a job to do.

6 Read this story, in which Cassy's father comes home, bringing some problems to the family. Then do the exercises that follow.

He came in the early morning, at about half past two. His feet padded along the balcony, slinking silently past the closed doors of the other flats. No one glimpsed his shadow, flickering across the curtain or noticed the uneven rhythm of his steps.

But he woke Cassy. She lay in her bed under the window and listened as the footsteps stopped outside. There were two quick, light taps ... like a signal.

Cassy sat up slowly. She heard the door of the back room open and Nan come hurrying out.

Wolf by Gillian Cross

a) Highlight the two short sentences.

b) The writer uses short sentences to draw the reader's attention to

Cassy   her father   Nan.

Circle the correct answer.

7 Read this extract, in which Simon deals with his anger. Do the exercises that follow.

a)

b)

c)

> Simon had had enough this time. Enough really did mean enough.
>
> He began by carefully tearing the pages from the open book on his desk. Next he opened up a wardrobe and pulled trousers, jumpers, t-shirts onto the floor. He ripped posters from the walls. He kicked over his lamp. He smashed the mirror. He shouted. He cried. He collapsed.

The short sentences in this story have different 'jobs'. Copy the correct label given here into the three boxes around the text.

bring the action to a close	emphasise a feeling	speed up the action

TIP

★ When you think you know *why* a short sentence is used, check that your idea fits in with the story.

8 Read this extract, in which two boy detectives find themselves in an unwanted fight.

The question hung in the air like a DVD on pause. The two friends looked at each other in horror. In a flash, they realised the terrible trap they had fallen into.

With only a moment's hesitation, Ashley threw himself like a battering ram against the first man. The second man raised his gun, but Finlay was too quick. Picking up a brick, he bashed it against the man's hand as hard as he could. Bones cracked.

Punches flew wildly, sending them all off balance and spilling off the pavement into the road. Cars swerved. Horns sounded. A bus glanced past. Fighting back was no longer on the minds of the two boys as they just tried to survive the traffic.

a) Highlight the short sentences.

b) Complete the sentences below to show what 'jobs' the short sentences are doing.

i) The writer has used the first short sentence to _____

_____ .

ii) The second group of short sentences is used to _____

_____ .

Level 4 readers can identify interesting language and make simple comments about it.
Level 5 readers can identify interesting language effects and make short comments about them.

TIP ★ You will need to **use your imagination** to work out 'extra' meanings in the choice of words.

What do you see?

The following technique is called **word association**. Use it to help you think about the reasons why a writer chooses a particular word.

9 What associations do you have with these words?

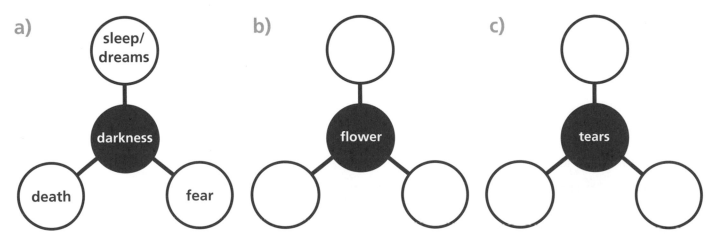

a)

sleep/dreams

darkness

death   fear

b)

flower

c)

tears

TIP ★ Use **word association** to help you think about why a writer chooses words.

10 This poem is about an unloved boy who sets fire to farm buildings and fields. The writer uses some interesting phrases to make the reader's brain work out another layer of detail in the poem.

a) What does the writer mean by burnt-out little eyes?

b) Why is the fire described as roaring hungrily?

c) How does a list help to describe the fire?

That one small boy with a face like pallid cheese
And burnt-out little eyes could make a blaze
As brazen, fierce and huge, as red and gold
And zany yellow as the one that spoiled
Three thousand guineas' worth of property
And crops at Godwin's Farm on Saturday
Is frightening – as fact and metaphor:
An ordinary match intended for
The lighting of a pipe or kitchen fire
Misused may set a whole menagerie
Of flame-fanged tigers roaring hungrily.
And frightening, too, that one small boy should set
The sky on fire and choke the stars to heat
Such skinny limbs and such a little heart
Which would have been content with one warm kiss
Had there been anyone to offer this.

Incendiary by Vernon Scannell

d Why has the writer used such twice here? Tick the correct answer.

★ To emphasise how small the boy is compared to the fire. ☐

★ Because he ran out of words. ☐

TIP ★ Look out for repetition. There is usually a reason for it.

Level 4 readers can recognise that a writer has used a list and make a simple comment about it.

Level 5 readers can recognise a list and suggest why the writer has used it.

Why do writers use lists?

There are two kinds of lists:

★ lists used to organise words so they can be seen easily;

★ lists used to build up words for an effect.

11 Read both versions of this story.

Which one do you like best? Why?

Once there was a boy who could walk on water.	Once there was a boy who could walk on water.
He lived with his grandfather and his mother on an island.	He lived with his grandfather and his mother on an island
The sea crept into the land with long twisting fingers.	where the sea crept into the land with long twisting fingers,
Rivers and streams wound round the island	and rivers and streams wound round and round and in and out between rocks and hills and fields
to make a patchwork of the land.	until the island was a patchwork sewn together with strips of shining water.

12 Fill the gaps with the words below.

The writer has used [a) _____] with round and round and in and out to make the pattern of the sentence [b) _____] the length of the rivers on the island. [c) _____] is used at rocks and hills and fields to show all the [d) _____] types of land on the island which [e) _____] the idea of it looking like a 'patchwork'.

| a list | different | lists and repetition | suggest | emphasises |

TIP

★ Look at how the list links to the sentences before and after it.

13 This story is set in a village in China long ago. A young girl is describing her lifestyle.

We never had much money, but I didn't really notice because neither did anyone else in our village. Father's favourite saying was, 'If you realise that you have enough, you are truly rich,' and he believed it. 'We have fresh food and warm clothes, a roof over our heads (a bit leaky when it rains) and a wooden bed to sleep on. What more can we ask for?' he demanded. 'And not only that,' he continued, 'but I have the finest little dumpling of a daughter in the whole of China.'   **a**

My parents worked hard to make sure that we always had enough. Father set off early in the morning, his farming tools over his shoulder, to tend the dozens of tiny terraces of vegetables that straggled higgledy-piggledy over the hillside above and below our house. He dug and sowed and weeded and cropped throughout the numbing cold of winter and the suffocating heat of summer. In the middle of the day, he returned home clutching triumphantly a gigantic sheaf of pak choi*, a basin of bright green beans, or a bucket full of melon-sized turnips.   **b**   **c**

* pak choi – Chinese cabbage

Spilled Water by Sally Grindley, Bloomsbury

SAMPLE QUESTION
Why has the writer used a list in **c**, the blue highlighted text part of the story?
SAMPLE ANSWER
The writer lists all the vegetables 'pak choi, a basin of bright green beans ...' to show how much food the father produced. The list emphasises that there was a lot of food, which is important as it seemed as if they were poor in other ways.

Explain why the writer has used the other two lists, **a** and **b**, highlighted in the story.

Identifying the writer's purpose

> Level 3 readers can identify the main purpose of a text.
> **Level 4 readers can identify and make simple comments about the purpose of a text.**

When you speak to people, you have an effect on them.

> Get out of here!

> I love you.

> And where is your homework this time?

It is the same with writing. Writers will think about the effect they want to have on the reader and then *choose* information and words to achieve this effect.

TIP

★ Imagine how the writer would read the words to you. What kind of voice would they use?

1   Read these short texts. What effect does the writer want to have on the reader? Choose from the words or phrases in the box below. There may be more than one correct answer!

a) The news is not good. We wait in hope … Join me tomorrow at 8.

b) If you want to join the Ambulance Service, you'll need five GCSEs and four years' driving experience.

c) If you are visiting Bahrain, stay at The Al Dana Resort Hotel with its private beach and heated outdoor pool. Try its famous international restaurant and then relax in its marble lounges.

d) He's new on the comedy circuit but, as far as I'm concerned, he has nothing new to amuse us.

inform	describe character	advise
persuade	amuse	
create suspense	give an opinion	

2 Read this story in which a girl has just seen her brother disappear under a mud slide. Then answer the questions that follow.

> I pounced through the creek to where he'd been standing and started scrabbling at the dirt, yelling out his name. The earth was heavy and sticky: my fingers left slick gouges behind them but hardly took anything away. I screeched to him over and over, thinking that if he could hear me he'd be comforted, all the while thrashing at the mud, spattering it into my hair and eyes and spitting it out with my cries.
>
> *Thursday's Child* by Sonya Hartnett

a) What is the writer trying to do in this text? Circle one of these phrases.

describe a character   create tension   give an opinion

b) What clues are there in the text to tell you that this is the writer's purpose?

_____

_____

3 Read this text, in which the writer focuses on car parking in Rome.

I love the way the Italians park. You turn any street corner in Rome and it looks as if you've just missed a parking competition for blind people. Cars are pointed in every direction, half on the pavements and half off, facing in, facing sideways, blocking garages and side streets and phone boxes, fitted into spaces so tight that the only possible way out would be through the sun roof.

Neither Here Nor There by Bill Bryson

a) What is the writer trying to do in this text? Circle one of these phrases.

advise   entertain   give information   give an opinion

b) What clues are there in the text to tell you that this is the writer's purpose?

_____

_____

_____

Level 3 readers can identify the main purpose of a text.
Level 4 readers can identify and make simple comments about the purpose of a text.

4 Find the pairs of speech bubbles with the same purpose and draw a line to link them with the purpose in the centre. One has been done for you.

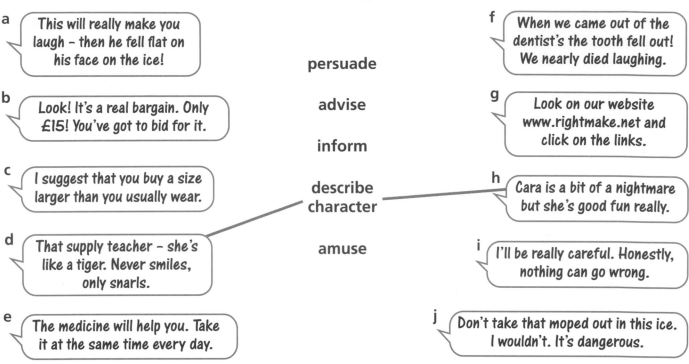

a (This will really make you laugh – then he fell flat on his face on the ice!)

f (When we came out of the dentist's the tooth fell out! We nearly died laughing.)

persuade

b (Look! It's a real bargain. Only £15! You've got to bid for it.)

advise

g (Look on our website www.rightmake.net and click on the links.)

inform

c (I suggest that you buy a size larger than you usually wear.)

describe character

h (Cara is a bit of a nightmare but she's good fun really.)

d (That supply teacher – she's like a tiger. Never smiles, only snarls.)

amuse

i (I'll be really careful. Honestly, nothing can go wrong.)

e (The medicine will help you. Take it at the same time every day.)

j (Don't take that moped out in this ice. I wouldn't. It's dangerous.)

> **TIP**
> ★ Read the texts aloud so you know what the writer *sounds* like.

5 Read this dialogue. Decide what the *purpose* of each speech is and fill in the number of the matching purpose given below in the box.

a) **Tania:** Jenny! Hugh's asked me to the cinema on Saturday. ☐

b) **Jenny:** Oh, go on Tania, say you'll go with him. Go on. ☐

c) **Tania:** It starts at 8.00 and finishes about half ten. He'll drive … ☐

d) **Jenny:** He's cool, Tania. Good looking. ☐ Got spikey dark hair and is tall and thin. ☐

e) **Tania:** Well, I might … but there again I might not. We'll have to see … ☐

f) **Jenny:** Look Tania, if I were you I'd go with him. That's what I'd do. You'll not get a better offer … ☐

1 giving an opinion	**4** creating suspense	**7** giving information
2 giving advice	**5** describing a character	
3 setting the scene	**6** persuading	

★   A writer may tell you only the good or only the bad about something. The writer is
    in control of what information you are given.

6   Read this text, which is from Roald Dahl's autobiography *Boy*. He writes about his first
experience of living away from home at St Peter's boarding school. Then use the words and
phrases from the box below to fill the gaps.

> I was homesick during the whole of my first term at St Peter's. Homesickness is a
> bit like seasickness. You don't know how awful it is till you get it, and when you do,
> it hits you right in the top of the stomach and you want to die.
>
> The only comfort is that both homesickness and seasickness are instantly curable.
> The first goes away the moment you walk out of the school grounds and the second
> is forgotten as soon as the ship enters port.

a) In the first paragraph, Roald Dahl wants the reader to _____.

b) He uses _____ and _____ to describe what
homesickness is like.

c) In the second paragraph, the writer wants to _____.

d) In both paragraphs, Roald Dahl wants to _____ the reader.

> entertain   exaggeration   comparison
> show that things get better   understand how awful he felt

TIP ★   Reading in the voice of the narrator or character will help you to recognise the
viewpoint.

7   Read this extract from a letter and do the exercises that follow.

> Dear Mum
> I wonder what you're having for tea tonight. Is it the usual Monday tea? My
> favourite? Shepherds Pie? I had a weird Spanish fishy thing. Pie Ella or
> something … Oh Mum, I sobbed myself to sleep last night. I feel awful, I hate
> it here. Can't I come home? I know you think I should try for longer but I am
> so miserable. Please let me come home. I don't think I can stand another two
> weeks here. I could paint the garden fence? Or get a job.

a) Circle three things the writer is trying to do.

   inform   amuse   persuade   create suspense

b) Highlight three phrases in the text and label them with your answers from **a**.

Level 4 readers can identify the purpose of a text.

Level 5 readers can identify the purpose of a text and begin to explain the effect of the text on the reader.

Reader – Who is it for?

Purpose – Why is it written?

I don't want to read that book. It's just for little kids!

Why do you say that?

It will make them laugh with all the silly jokes and characters, but not me.

8 Read these short texts and complete the table below. The first one is done for you.

a) Pelling Cricket Club. New members welcome. Come along to nets on a Tuesday at 7 p.m. We run two Saturday League teams and a Sunday friendly side. The Club runs various events throughout the year, including a Race Night, a Quiz and a Dinner Dance.

b) Peter Kay is, without doubt, one of Britain's funniest and best-loved comedians. And for the first time in his own words, he tells us how he came to achieve his extraordinary success and the hilarious journey that got him there.

c) Hearing Dogs are asking for volunteers to run in a charity event, with their dogs or their friends' dogs, to raise money to train more 'Hearing Dogs'. They need funds and they need to find dog lovers prepared to foster a dog during its training. They hope this event, in September this year, will do both.

d) Wire Chair   £123

Try this polished steel design if you want to give your dining area a space-age look. It is more comfortable than it looks and with a clear glass table, looks stunning.

	Where might you find this text?	**Who is it written for? READER**	**Why has it been written? PURPOSE**
a)	Local newspaper/notice outside the club	People interested in cricket	To encourage new people to join the club
b)			
c)			
d)			

TIP ★ Imagine the text in real-life situations to help you.

There is often a **main purpose**, and then **other purposes** within a text.

9 This text is from a letter about school trips for KS3.

> ## We hope to answer some of your questions below.
>
> **1**
> Is there a choice of trips?
>
> Yes, there is:
> - a football tournament in Spain;
> - an activity holiday in Derbyshire;
> - an orchestra trip to Holland;
> - an art department trip to Italy.
>
> **2**
> Will my child be in any danger on a school trip?
> We do everything we can to ensure that your child is not in danger. We have clear safety policies and there is a member of staff whose job it is to make sure your children are safe. The school's priority on any trip is safety.
>
> **3**
> Is our money spent well?
> We stay in clean, comfortable accommodation, but not in luxury. We eat well, but simply. We make sure that the trips are good value for money.
>
> **4**
> What if we can't afford to pay for a trip?
> If a trip is more expensive than you can afford, we will help with the cost.

a) Who is the intended READER? Circle the correct answer.

teacher   children   parents

b) What is the purpose of the **whole** text? Tick the correct answer.

★ To give information about the next school trip. ☐

★ To offer to meet the cost of school trips. ☐

★ To persuade them to go on school trips. ☐

★ To persuade parents to let their children join in school trips. ☐

c) What is the purpose of each section of the text?

Write the number of each section in the boxes to identify the purpose of each section.

explains how children will be protected ☐

gives information about costs ☐

lists the different trips ☐

describes conditions on the trips ☐

When you have identified the purpose of a text, it is important to give an explanation and evidence for your ideas.

In these tasks, you will practise giving explanations for your ideas.

10 In this story, a Siamese cat and dog who have lost their owners are making their way across Canada to try to find them.

Here, they have arrived at a river …

> The poor cat now showed the first signs of fear since leaving on his journey: he was alone, and the only way to rejoin his friends lay in swimming across the terrible stretch of water. He ran up and down the bank, all the time keeping up his unearthly Siamese wailing. The young dog went through the same tiring performance that he had used before, swimming to and fro, trying to entice him into the water; but the cat was beside himself with terror and it was a long time before he finally made up his mind. When he did it was with a sudden blind desperate rush at the water, completely un-catlike. His expression of horror and distaste was almost comical as he started swimming towards the young dog who waited for him a few yards out. He proved to be a surprisingly good swimmer, and was making steady progress across, the dog swimming alongside, when tragedy struck.
>
> *The Incredible Journey* by Sheila Burnford

a) What are the writer's purposes? Tick True or False.

The writer wants the audience to:

i)   see how dangerous the situation is.   **True** ☐   **False** ☐

ii) think of the dog as a hero.   **True** ☐   **False** ☐

iii) think that the cat is a coward.   **True** ☐   **False** ☐

iv) understand the cat's fear.   **True** ☐   **False** ☐

b) Highlight the evidence in the text for each of the purposes you have marked as True.

Any of these answers could be true. At Level 5 it is important that you give a **reason** for your opinion.

c) Continue the answer below to explain **how** the writer achieves these **purposes**.

The writer has several purposes in this section of the story. The main purpose is to

_____. She achieves this by _____.

d) Look at the last sentence. How does the writer want the reader to feel at this point? Circle one.

relieved   **surprised**   **amused**   **sad**   **disappointed**

11 This story is set in America, a long time ago. In this section, Tom has a loose tooth. His aunt has an interesting way of pulling it out.

'Your tooth, indeed! What's the matter with your tooth?'

'One of them's loose, and it aches perfectly awful.'

'There, there now, don't begin that groaning again. Open your mouth. Well, your tooth *is* loose, but you're not going to die about that. Mary, get me a silk thread, and a chunk of fire out of the kitchen.'

Tom said:
'Oh, please, Auntie, don't pull it out, it don't hurt any more. I wish I may never stir if it does. Please don't, Auntie, I don't want to stay home from school.'

'Oh, you don't, don't you? So all this row was because you thought you'd get to stay home from school and go a fishing? Tom, Tom, I love you so, and you seem to try every way you can to break my old heart with your outrageousness.'

By this time the dental instruments were ready. The old lady made one end of the silk thread fast to Tom's tooth with a loop and tied the other to the bed-post. Then she seized the chunk of fire and suddenly thrust it almost into the boy's face. The tooth hung dangling by the bedpost, now.

The Adventures of Tom Sawyer by Mark Twain

Complete this paragraph to explain how the writer presents the relationship between Tom and his aunt.

The writer shows that Auntie has a good **a)** [   ] of Tom. We can

see this when she realises that Tom is just trying to avoid going to school.

However, the writer shows that she is **b)** [   ] of Tom when she

says, 'I love you so.' Auntie is also presented as a **c)** [   ] and

d) [   ] person when she pulls out the tooth.

| tough | fond | understanding | determined |

12 a) PURPOSE: Does the writer want this story to seem funny, frightening, cruel or educational?

b) HOW is the PURPOSE achieved?
Answer this question by highlighting two points in the story and explaining HOW they help the overall purpose.

Pages 6–9: Finding information in a text (L3–4)

1 breathe; smell; pick up (food); suck up water
2 African elephant: fan-shaped ears; ears up to 1.5 metres wide; two lips on trunk
Asian elephant: one lip on trunk; triangular ears; smaller type of elephant
3 Jackal eats: fruit, grasses, dead flesh;
Fennec fox eats: lizards, insects
4 a) no b) kitchen stool c) a fox d) left/went out
5 a) university b) quick c) cheap d) flour e) salt
6 a) i) turkey curry ii) broccoli iii) apple
b) i) chargrilled peppers and baked onions in a tomato pasta
ii) baby new carrots with parsley
iii) banana ice cream with chocolate sauce
7 Charlie: Hot and Spicy
Abdul: Cheese and Tomato
Tom: Three Cheese
Nick: Hot and Spicy
8 a) under 16 b) fat, salt, sugar c) 39 million
d) junk food, 9

Pages 10–13: Finding information in a text (L4–5)

9 a) UK's biggest and best; delivering DVDs to your door; games and a downloads service; try the service for free; watch as many DVDs as you like; free postage both ways; no late fees
b) lots of people use it; convenient; more than just DVDs; no cost to try it first; no decisions to make; easy/cheap to return; no worrying about when it's due back
10 a) *Any four from:*

Change	Evidence
stopped smoking	gave up smoking
got fit/took up exercise/training	exercised five times a week
cut down on alcohol	stopped drinking beer every day
got his body in shape	as for looking good – he achieved that too!
worked with a trainer	His trainer was …
did stunts and fights	This wasn't his normal work.

b) look good (like a James Bond); to be able to do the fights and stunts in the film
11 a) science class; canteen
b) nearly blew up science lab; dropped a tray of food; slipped on beans
c) swing; roundabout; slide; tyre
12 a) i) Sun and Sand
ii) 24 August in Sheffield Hallam Arena
iii) 29 November in Chicago
iv) £35
v) 1.1 million or more
vi) 'Emotional Avenue'
b) *Highlight the above information in the article.*
c) *Check your answer with your teacher.*

Pages 14–17: Understanding what the writer 'suggests' (L3–4)

1 a) sad; disappointed b) old; injured
c) lazy; crafty
2 a) angry b) is pleased about something
c) about to attack

3 a) True: luckily it wasn't
b) False: seriously no good
c) True: calls everyone 'dude'
d) True: excellent coach/My game has really improved.
4 a) entertaining; applauding; cheering
b) the joker of the tennis world; the clown prince
5 a) charged (up the steps)/piled out
b) beamed c) over at last
6 Don't rush because you have plenty of time in a day's visit.
7 teeth showing in a snarl
8 a) doesn't really want
b) shock her parents/(mother's question) was almost more than she could bear/quivering lips
c) used to her
d) clues that tell you they are not reacting to her with shock but very normally, as if running away were a perfectly natural thing to do: enquired Ramona's mother politely; neither spoke
e) almost more than Ramona could bear; quivering lips
f) heartless
9 Look for words and phrases that give you clues/evidence.

Pages 18–21: Understanding what the writer 'suggests' (L4–5)

10 a) i) False ii) False iii) True iv) True
b) *Highlight any of the evidence which you think is true.*
c) *Check your answer with your teacher.*
11 a)

	The writer suggests he …	Evidence from the text
Bert	fancies Bella	dreamily, his eyes firmly fixed on number seven.
	stands up to Wayne	Well, there you're wrong.
Wayne	knows best/likes to be right is sarcastic	It was good to be right, for once. Wayne sarcastically
	thinks girls can't play football	This is going to be rubbish/Wayne stared at Bella in disbelief/Not bad for a girl.
	finds Spanish lessons dull	as gripping as a Spanish lesson

b) *Check your answer with your teacher.*
12 a) i) True ii) False iii) True iv) False v) True
b) *Highlight any of the evidence which you think is true.*
13 a) They taste great!: sense of humour/likes to shock/is a joker
complained: moans/always finds problems/is a complainer
she would report him: can't take a joke/falls for tricks/likes to be correct and proper
he would buy her a sense of humour: thinks she is too serious/is puzzled she doesn't understand him
b) *Check your answer with your teacher.*

Pages 22–25: Commenting on the organisation of texts (L3–4)

1 a) title b) subtitle c) love life
d) action – what to do

2 *Show this to your teacher.*

3 title: quickly catches reader's attention; para 1: describes suffering; para 2: asks for money; para 3: offers hope; para 4: gives a promise

4 *Show this to your teacher.*

5 *Give your opinion.*

6 a) First of all, he describes **the movements and the fun**. Then he tells you **he was sick**.

b) First of all, she describes **being sick**. Then she tells you **about the movements and how it was fun on the rides**.

c) *Your own answer with a reason.*

7 a)/b) *Show this to your teacher.*

8 a) father **b)** mother

c) He wants to show someone else's reaction to the father/the event.

9 a) Mama handed him the passports and smiled. But the hand with which she was holding her handbag was squeezing it into terrible contortions.

b) It brings tension/danger to the text./Without the sentences, nothing exciting or dangerous would be shown.

Pages 26–29: Commenting on the organisation of texts (L4–5)

10 a)–e) True

11 a) summary **b)** cliff hanger **c)** request

12 a) cliff hanger

b) We want to know what will happen next.

c) The start mentions the 'market' in a shocking way so you want to read on. The ending also mentions the market and you still want to know more.

d) To show her character and suggest how she is affected by the events to show the horror of the situation.

13

Paragraph number	Statistical evidence	Real-life examples	Other
1	✓		
2	✓		
3		✓	
4		✓	
5	✓		
6		✓	
7			✓

14 Summarises the content.

15 So readers can relate figures to real life.

16 It asks/requests that people do something to prevent the problem mentioned in the first paragraph.

17 Statistics – duller to read – shorter, punchy paragraphs
Real-life events – interesting stories – in longer paragraphs

Pages 30–33: Commenting on how a writer uses language for effect (L3–4)

1 desperate/worried/devastated.
Check your answers with your teacher.

2 Positive: well-dressed; smart pin-stripe suit
Negative: small, piggy eyes; frayed; stained
Neutral: button nose; still unread; anxiously

3 a) **bullying** as stronger/more deliberate than **bossy**

b) **house** is just a building, **home** is a good place to be/live

4 *Check your answers with your teacher.*

5 a) Suggests that the cold air is more dangerous/capable of killing.

b) Suggests how sharp/cutting/painful the wind is.

6 a) But he woke Cassy. Cassy sat up slowly.

b) Cassy

7 a) speed up the action

b) emphasise a feeling

c) bring the action to a close

8 a) Bones cracked. Cars swerved. Horns sounded. A bus glanced past.

b) i) highlight the noise

ii) show lots of different things happening all around them

Pages 34–37: Commenting on how a writer uses language for effect (L4–5)

9 a)–c) *Check your diagrams with your teacher.*

10 a) it makes it sound like they have seen a lot of things and are dead

b) it makes it sound like a creature

c) builds up the effect of lots of flames/speed

d) To emphasise how small the boy is compared to the fire.

11 *Give your opinions with reasons why.*

12 a) lists and repetition **b)** suggest **c)** A list

d) different **e)** emphasises

13 *Check your answer with your teacher.*

Pages 38–41: Identifying the writer's purpose (L3–4)

1 a) inform/create suspense **b)** inform

c) advise/persuade **d)** give an opinion

2 a) create tension

b) words such as screeched, scrabbling; thrashing

3 a) entertain

b) parking competition for blind people; the only possible way out would be through the sun roof.

4 a, f: amuse
b, i: persuade
c, j: advise
e, g: inform

5 a) 3 setting the scene

b) 6 persuading

c) 7 giving information

d) 1 giving an opinion & 5 describing a character

e) 4 creating suspense

f) 2 giving advice

6 a) understand how awful he felt

b) exaggeration, comparison

c) show that things get better

d) entertain

7 a) inform, amuse, persuade

b) *inform*: I sobbed myself to sleep last night. I feel awful, I hate it here./I had a weird Spanish fishy thing
amuse: Pie Ella or something …/Or get a job
persuade: Can't I come home? Please let me come home
Check with your teacher if you think you have found another correct one.

Pages 42–45: Identifying the writer's purpose (L4–5)

8

	Where might you find this text?	Who is it written for? READER	Why has it been written? PURPOSE
a)	Local newspaper/notice outside the club	People interested in cricket	To encourage new people to join the club
b)	Book cover/ review	Fans of Peter Kay	Persuade people to buy
c)	Newspaper/ noticeboard	Dog lovers/ runners	Ask for support/ advertise event
d)	Catalogue/ magazine	Home owners	Persuade people to buy

9   **a)** parents
     b) To persuade parents to let their children join in school trips.
     c) 2 4 1 3

10 **a)** **i)** True **ii)** True **iii)** True **iv)** True
     b) *Check your answers with your teacher.*
     c) *Check your answer with your teacher.*
     d) surprised

11 **a)** understanding **b)** fond **c)** tough/determined
     d) tough/determined

12 **a)** *All answers could be correct.*
     b) *Check your answer with your teacher.*